WIND & ROOT
PRESS
WWW.WINDANDROOT.CA

FROM SCHOENAU

A true story.

For Robbie and Ben.

Written and illustrated by
ANDREA GIBB

www.andreagibb.com @andrea_gibb_author

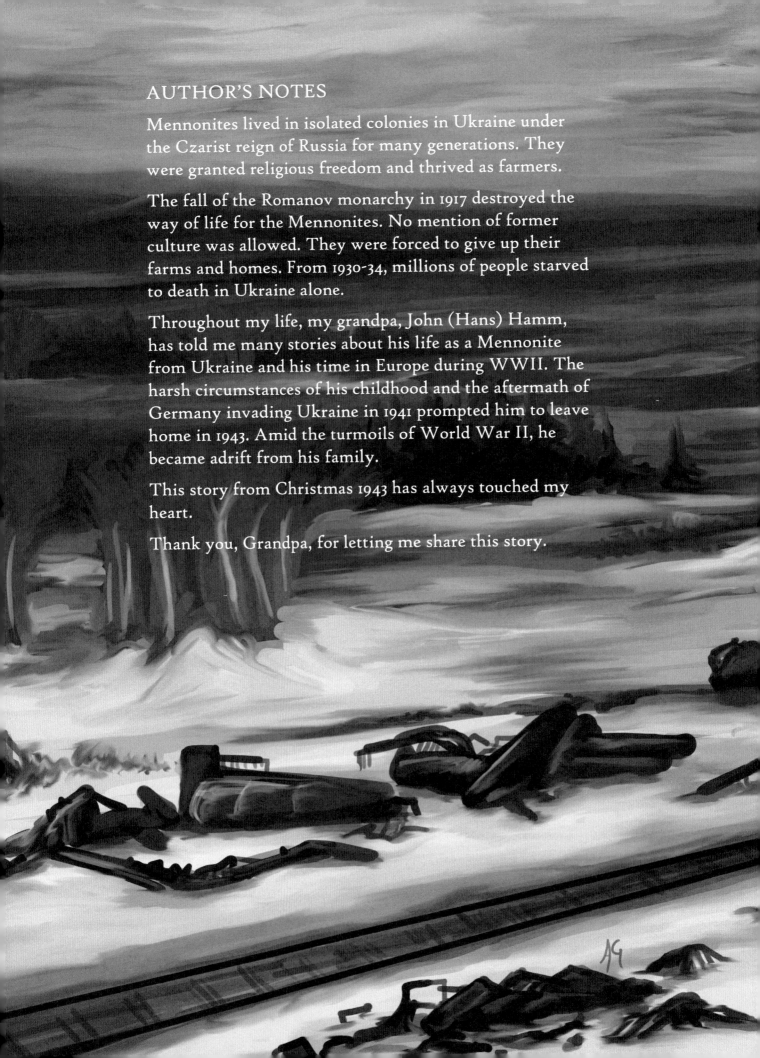

AUTHOR'S NOTES

Mennonites lived in isolated colonies in Ukraine under the Czarist reign of Russia for many generations. They were granted religious freedom and thrived as farmers.

The fall of the Romanov monarchy in 1917 destroyed the way of life for the Mennonites. No mention of former culture was allowed. They were forced to give up their farms and homes. From 1930-34, millions of people starved to death in Ukraine alone.

Throughout my life, my grandpa, John (Hans) Hamm, has told me many stories about his life as a Mennonite from Ukraine and his time in Europe during WWII. The harsh circumstances of his childhood and the aftermath of Germany invading Ukraine in 1941 prompted him to leave home in 1943. Amid the turmoils of World War II, he became adrift from his family.

This story from Christmas 1943 has always touched my heart.

Thank you, Grandpa, for letting me share this story.

FROM SCHOENAU

A true story.

I sit in the train car, my arms and legs tucked in to keep my skin from touching the metal that is colder than ice. Flakes of snow leap into the train car as the wind rushes by.

Like ghosts, echoes of voices ride the winter wind, following us all the way back from the swamps of White Russia.

I curl my toes inside my shoes trying to keep them warm.
It is December 1943.
I am fourteen years old.

The train rumbles, jolting along the track in the night. The rough motion makes me shudder. I think of all the train cars that did not escape the graveyard that is the Pripet Marsh.

Some officers believe boys should not be on the front lines of war. They think us Volksdeutche boys from the Ukraine should experience Weihnachten, German Christmas, for the first time.

I am assigned to a small village where I stay with a kind family.
They live in an apartment filled with beautiful furniture. As the
house is aired out, lovely, bright curtains sway in the crisp winter
breeze. I sleep in a bed with a white feather blanket so soft it almost
smothers me. And in the morning for breakfast, Frau feeds me big
puffy kernels of wheat and with milk poured on top.

My accent sounds coarse next to their elegant German. No wonder
we are called Volksdeutsche. I vow *never* to blow my nose onto the
floor again.

I help the village toymaker with the toys for Christmas,
brushing lacquer or sanding.

For lunch, Frau packs me a sandwich wrapped like
a present.

I am asked to go to the neighboring village and dress as Saint Nikolaus and give out toys to the children at the Burgermiester's Christmas party.

I heave the sack of toys over my shoulder and board the train.

When the train arrives at the station, the daylight is almost gone.
The snow is thick and heavy and everything is hushed. I can't
imagine any vehicle can get through the deep snow from the
station to the village.

I notice two boxcars parked on the sideline. Out of the cars come refugees, a common enough sight. These are like the others I've seen, huddling together for warmth, their clothing basically rags, not a proper coat or shoe between them.

Dusk is settling.

I have somewhere to be.

Soon it will be dark dark dark.

I adjust the sack on my shoulder and make my way under the archway of snow-laden trees to the village.

At the Burgermeister's house, they welcome me and help me dress as Saint Nikolaus, and tell me how to play the part. With the sack over my shoulder (and a stick tucked in it for the naughty ones), I enter a room full of children.

I ask if they have been naughty or nice. Then I hand out toys
until the sack is empty.

Then everyone sings. Beautiful songs fill the house. I
have never heard Christmas music before. I don't know
the words, but I listen and I feel the music chase away the
dark of winter.

The Burgermeister's wife asks me, "Where are your parents?"

"I don't know," I tell her.

When the party is over, I head back to the train station. Everything is so quiet.

A stooped figure walks toward me, shuffling through the deep snow. We pass. Her tattered coat does not hide her legs wrapped in rags.

I should have looked back or said something, but I have a train to catch and the night is cold and dark and lonely.

Back at Frau's house, more songs are sung. I am given a pair
of hand-knitted mittens.

My first Christmas gift.

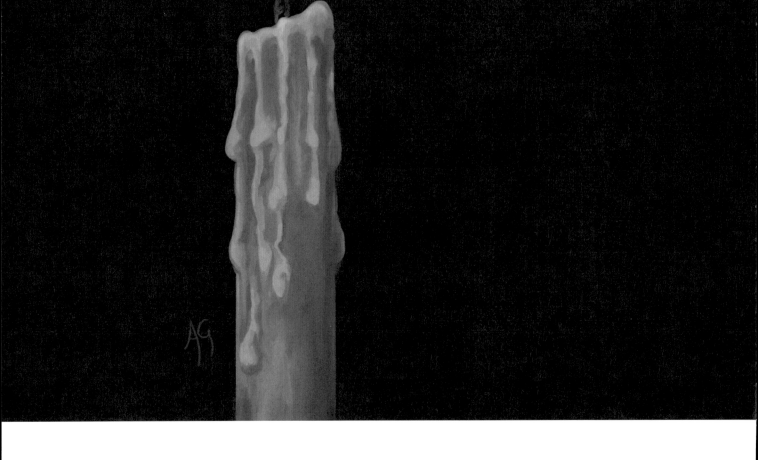

Then to preserve light for another night,

the candles are extinguished.

The next morning, the sun glistens. The crisp air beckons all
to find skis or sleds. I am free to have fun in the snow with the
other children.

A telegram comes from the Burgermeister:

I am to go back.

Immediately.

As I ride the train, I worry I have done something wrong.

I walk the same way as the night before and the avenue of trees
is noble and tall and the snow is white white white.

When I arrive, the Burgermeister's wife greets me. She is so nice, my worries disappear. But she asks me again, "You are Hans Hamm?"

"Yes," I reply.

"You are from Ukraine?"

"Yes, yes."

"From the village of Schoenau?"

"Yes. Yes. Yes."

Satisfied by my answers, she takes me to the next room where
a woman waits. A woman wearing a tattered coat, her legs
wrapped with rags. The woman I passed along the long lonely
road the night before.

"Hans, this woman is from your village of Schoenau!" Frau tells me.

Of course, I know that now. The woman in the tattered coat is my mother. *How* had I not recognized her?

Mother is one of the refugees from the train. She had gone to the Burgermeister for help and told them she was from the village of Schoenau.

Not only did they help her, but they remembered the boy
who played Saint Nikolaus (me, of course!) who was from
that **same village!**

It's winter and the wind howls and sings its sad song, but my mother holds me close, closer than ever before and her love settles inside my heart . . .

. . . and warms me right down to my toes.

The end.